UQ AI

The Key to Intelligent
Parameterization in AI

KATIA DORIA FONSECA VASCONCELOS

Dedication:

To my beloved children, Mario (Teik), Bruna, Victor, and Bárbara, who are the inspiration and reason behind my relentless pursuit of knowledge. You are my strength and motivation to share my ideas and experiences.

To my husband José de Vasconcelos Filho, whose collaboration and support have been instrumental in the creation of this book. Your unwavering dedication and support are a precious gift in my life.

To my dear grandchildren, Davi, Vivi, and João Gabriel, who represent the continuation of our stories and the hope for a bright future. May this book inspire you to explore your passions and seek truth in all things.

To my sons-in-law and daughters-in-law, Nikolas Bucvar, Eduardo, Jana, and Jacque, who strengthen our family with their love, support, and valuable contributions.

I am grateful for being part of this journey and for sharing your perspectives and enriching experiences.

May this be dedicated to all of you, my beloved family, with all my love and gratitude.

Katia Doria Fonseca Vasconcelos

INTRODUCTION:

Welcome to the book "UQ IA: The Key to Semantic Intelligent Parametrization of AI". In this work, we will explore the intersection between the principles of UQ (Universal Quotient) and semantic parametrization in the field of Artificial Intelligence (AI). We will embark on a fascinating journey that will lead us to understand how the strategic application of UQ can drive the efficiency and effectiveness of AI algorithms.

AI has played an increasingly relevant role in our world, transforming the way we live, work, and relate. However, to unlock the full potential of AI, it is essential to consider not only the technical aspects but also the understanding and incorporation of fundamental human principles.

This is where UQ comes into play. UQ is a holistic approach that values the balance and harmony between different dimensions of human intelligence, including 360-degree vision, adaptability, synchronicity, resilience, and emotional control. By applying these principles to the semantic parametrization of AI algorithms, we are able to create smarter systems that better understand and meet the needs of users, project teams, and even entire organizations.

In this book, we will delve deep into each of these UQ principles and how they can be incorporated into the semantic parametrization of AI. You will find a thorough analysis of the theoretical foundations, practical examples, and insights on how to apply these concepts in different contexts. Additionally, we will discuss the challenges and opportunities that arise when using the UQ approach in intelligent AI parametrization.

Whether you are an AI enthusiast, a professional in the field, a team leader, or simply someone interested in exploring the revolutionary potential of AI, this book is for you. Get ready for an exciting journey into the future of AI, where balance and human understanding play a central role in intelligent parametrization.

Let's dive together into the world of UQ IA and uncover the secrets of this innovative approach that is transforming AI into an even more powerful and meaningful tool.

Happy learning!

TABLE OF CONTENTS:

PRESENTATION OF THE UQ CONCEPT: UNIVERSAL SYNCHRONIC INTELLIGENCE QUOTIENT

Human success is driven by the balance of UQ (Universal Synchronic Intelligence Quotient), a concept supported by scientific research and case studies. Several studies have explored the aspects of UQ and its effects in different areas of human life.

A study conducted by researchers at Stanford University revealed the importance of developing resilience and emotional control in achieving positive outcomes in careers and relationships.

10

This research demonstrated how the ability to cope with adversity and control emotions contributes to making informed decisions and building healthy and productive relationships.

Clayton Christensen, renowned professor of Business Administration at Harvard, emphasizes that disruptive innovation requires a change in approach and the overcoming of outdated paradigms. He highlights that success lies in embracing change and quickly adapting to new circumstances.

Daniel Kahneman, psychologist and Nobel laureate economist, reminds us that our decisions are influenced by how we perceive problems. By adopting a positive perspective and seeing challenges as opportunities for learning, we can make better decisions and achieve superior results. The theory of emotional intelligence, developed by Daniel Goleman, also aligns with the concept of UQ, emphasizing the importance of emotional balance for personal and professional success.

Howard Gardner, renowned psychologist and professor at the Harvard Graduate School of Education, highlights the importance of balancing and developing all our intelligences. He encourages us to reprogram our educational approach, valuing not only logical-mathematical intelligence but also emotional, musical, spatial, and other intelligences, allowing us to explore our full potential.

These influential figures, along with other proponents of innovative thinking, reinforce the importance of adopting a new perspective when facing problems. By balancing our potentials through 360-degree vision, resilience, adaptability, synchronicity, and emotional control, we are prepared to face challenges with confidence, creativity, and effectiveness. This approach also relates to other relevant theories and concepts, such as

Carol Dweck's growth mindset, which emphasizes the importance of a growth mindset in the pursuit of success.

In this book, we will comprehensively explore the principles of UQ and how they relate to different areas of human life. We will analyze scientific research, inspiring case studies, and relevant theories to provide a broad and well-founded understanding of the balance of UQ and its impact on personal and professional success.

Now, let's dive into the exploration of the five principles of UQ: 360-degree Vision, Resilience, Adaptability,

Synchronicity, and Emotional Control. Each of these principles plays a fundamental role in the pursuit of balance and the development of your potentials.

360-degree Vision: 360-degree Vision involves having a broad and comprehensive perspective on all dimensions of your life. It is the ability to see beyond the obvious, to understand the interconnections between different areas, and to identify opportunities that others may not perceive. In challenges related to 360-degree Vision, you will be stimulated to explore different angles and consider various perspectives to make informed decisions.

Resilience: Resilience is the ability to cope with adversity, overcome obstacles, and quickly recover from challenging situations. It is the skill to adapt to change and keep moving forward, even in the face of difficulties. In challenges of Resilience, you will be challenged to face difficult situations, learn from them, and find ways to strengthen yourself in the face of adversity.

Adaptability: Adaptability is the ability to adjust and adapt to different circumstances and demands. It is the capacity to be flexible, open to change, and willing to experiment with new approaches. In challenges of Adaptability, you will be challenged to step out of your comfort zone, try new ways of doing things, and adapt to changes in your environment.

Emotional Control: Emotional Control involves the ability to manage your emotions effectively, especially in pressure and stressful situations. It is the skill to stay calm, make rational decisions, and deal with challenges in a balanced manner. In challenges of Emotional Control, you will be challenged to recognize your emotions, develop strategies to deal with them, and maintain emotional balance in challenging situations.

Synchronicity: Synchronicity refers to the harmony and coordination of your actions within the environment you are in. It is the ability to synchronize your tasks, projects, and goals to achieve an efficient and effective workflow. In challenges of Synchronicity, you will be challenged to organize your activities, establish priorities, and find ways to optimize your time and resources.

Throughout this book, we will explore each of these principles in detail, presenting practical challenges, reflective questions, and exercises that will help you develop your skills and balance your potentials.

Get ready for a journey of self-discovery, personal growth, and the full activation of your UQ! Remember, the balance of these principles is crucial to achieve extraordinary results in all areas of your life. Let's explore, challenge, and develop the best in you. We are excited to accompany you on this transformative journey!

PRACTICAL EXAMPLE: PARAMETRIZING AI WITH UQ PRINCIPLES

In this chapter, we will explore a practical example of how parametrization of Artificial Intelligence (AI) based on UQ principles can be effectively applied. We will follow the case of an e-commerce company aiming to enhance customer service by offering a personalized experience aligned with UQ values.

The company implemented an AI system that utilizes a neural network to process customer interactions. Through this system, the company seeks to apply UQ principles such as 360-degree vision, adaptability, emotional control, resilience, and synchronicity to provide more comprehensive and customer-oriented service.

In the practical example, a new customer visits the company's website and fills out a form with their preferences, interests, and personal information. This data is sent to the neural network, which performs pre-processing and checks for ethical aspects, security, privacy, fairness, among others, according to UQ principles.

Next, the data is directed to the hidden layer of the neural network, where analysis and categorization of the information take place. The machine identifies the customer's tone of expression, evaluating their level of urgency, emotional state, and expectations. Based on this analysis, the AI generates a personalized response, such as product recommendations or relevant information for the customer.

Throughout the interaction, both the machine and the customer provide real-time feedback. This feedback is essential for adjusting and optimizing the parameters of the neural network, always striving for a balance between

UQ principles. Over time, the AI becomes more adaptable and accurate in understanding the customer's needs, and the customer becomes accustomed to the personalized and efficient service provided by the machine.

This practical example demonstrates how parametrization of AI with UQ principles can transform the customer experience and drive results for a company. By applying these principles in a structured and conscious manner, it is possible to achieve a balance between human understanding and the machine's capacity for learning and decision-making.

In the next chapter, we will delve even deeper into the role of intelligent parametrization based on UQ principles, exploring advanced techniques and use cases in different contexts.

We hope that this practical example inspires and assists you in implementing intelligent parametrization of AI aligned with UQ principles in your own project or company.

To simplify the illustration of how this parametrization approach works in a neural network, we can depict the process as follows:

Data Input: The system receives input data, which can

be information provided by a customer in a form, for example.

Pre-processing: The input data undergoes pre-processing, where ethical aspects, security, privacy, fairness, among others, are checked. This step ensures that the data aligns with UQ principles.

Hidden Layer: The pre-processed data is sent to the hidden layer of the neural network. In this layer, data analysis and categorization occur, considering aspects such as synchronicity, emotional control, and adaptability.

Tone of Expression: The neural network identifies the customer's tone of expression, which may indicate urgency, stress, calmness, among others. This contributes to adapting the service and improving synchronicity between the machine and the customer.

Personalized Response: Based on the data analysis and tone of expression, the neural network generates a personalized response, such as a quote, a product recommendation, or any other desired interaction.

Feedback and Adjustments: The interaction with the

customer continues, and the neural network receives real-time feedback. This feedback is used to adjust and optimize the parameters of the neural network, always seeking a balance between UQ principles.

Joint Cognition: Throughout the interaction, both the machine and the customer adjust and learn, creating a form of joint cognition where the machine better understands the customer's needs and expectations, and the customer adapts to the machine's mode of service.

This is a simplified view of how this parametrization approach based on UQ principles could work in a neural network. It is important to note that in practice, the implementation would be more complex and involve the use of machine learning algorithms, natural language processing techniques, among other aspects.

Expanding Model Capacity with UQ Incorporation and Weighted Machine Learning

Before we delve into the incorporation of UQ and the use of weights to expand the capacity of machine learning models, it is important to understand the significance of having more comprehensive and contextual models. These models can capture crucial aspects of human behavior and intelligently apply them to data generation and discrimination, resulting in more accurate and relevant predictions.

UQ Incorporation: By adding additional layers of information and processing to the neural network, we enrich the model with UQ principles. However, UQ incorporation requires specific preprocessing techniques and strategies to appropriately represent and incorporate this information. Additionally, it is necessary to have properly annotated or labeled datasets, including the desired UQ information.

Weighted Usage: Weights play a crucial role in incorporating UQ into machine learning models. They allow for adjusting the importance of different features and influencing how the model processes and analyzes data. For example, we can adjust weights to emphasize certain UQ information, such as individual preferences, and weigh different features, such as genre, cast, director, among others, to enhance the accuracy of predictions.

Application Example: Let's explore a practical example to illustrate how UQ incorporation and weighted usage can be applied in a movie recommendation model. In this case, UQ is utilized to personalize recommendations based on users' individual interests and preferences, while weights are used to adjust the importance of different characteristics. This leads to more accurate and relevant predictions, enabling the model to offer personalized recommendations according to each user's needs.

Considerations and Challenges: Although UQ incorporation and weighted usage have significant benefits, it is important to mention some challenges and considerations to take into account. The availability and quality of UQ data can be limitations, as well as the computational complexity and implementation cost of these approaches. It is crucial to evaluate these factors before applying UQ incorporation and weighted usage in a machine learning model.

Conclusion: UQ incorporation and weighted usage are powerful approaches to expand the capacity of machine learning models. By applying these concepts, it is possible to capture crucial aspects of human behavior and enrich models with contextual information. This results in more accurate, relevant, and personalized predictions, improving the user experience and driving results in various application contexts.

ACTIVATION FUNCTIONS, BIAS, AND UQ INTEGRATION: ADJUSTING BEHAVIOR AND BALANCE IN NEURAL NETWORKS

In this chapter, we will explore activation functions, bias, and UQ integration in the intelligent parametrization of neural networks. These elements play a crucial role in adjusting the behavior and balance of the neural network, enabling the incorporation of UQ principles such as 360-degree vision, adaptability, synchronicity, resilience, and emotional control.

Activation Functions:

Each neural unit in a layer can have an associated activation function, which defines its behavior in relation to input signals. There are several common activation functions, such as the sigmoid function, the Rectified Linear Unit (ReLU) function, and the SoftMax function. In the context of UQ and intelligent parametrization of AI, the choice of activation function can be made to promote balance and desired principles. For example, an activation function that incorporates resilience, adaptability, and emotional control characteristics can be selected to influence the behavior of neurons.

Bias:

Bias refers to an additional parameter added to each neural unit in a layer. It allows for adjusting the behavior of the neural unit, in addition to the synaptic connections and associated weights. The use of bias in neural networks is a common and important practice to increase the flexibility and learning capacity of the model. Bias enables the neural network to adapt and learn patterns even when all inputs are zero, contributing to the balance and adjustment of network behavior.

UQ Integration: UQ can be integrated into the architecture of the neural network, adjusting and parametrizing the network according to UQ principles such as 360-degree vision, adaptability, synchronicity, resilience, and emotional control. Similar to how bias adjusts the behavior of neural units, UQ can be used to balance the machine's behavior with the desired human principles. Parametrizing the neural network based on UQ principles aims to create an architecture that incorporates desired features of balance and synchronous intelligence, facilitating better interaction between the machine and the human.

Bias Adjustment Example:

To illustrate bias adjustment, let's consider an image classification model that needs to recognize and distinguish different types of animals. By properly adjusting the bias, we can balance the behavior of the model, avoiding biased classifications towards certain types of animals, ensuring a fair and balanced approach.

Conclusion:

Activation functions, bias, and UQ integration play crucial roles in building neural networks that promote balance between the machine and the human. These elements allow for adjusting the behavior of neural units, modeling complex relationships in data, and incorporating UQ principles into the intelligent parametrization of AI. Through these adjustments, the goal is to create more efficient, accurate, and adaptable neural networks capable of harmoniously meeting needs and expectations.

Matrices and Architecture of UQ: Representing and Parameterizing Neural Networks Based on UQ Principles

In this chapter, we will discuss the relevant matrices in neural network projects and machine learning algorithms, with a focus on parameterization based on UQ principles. Additionally, we will explore the UQ architecture and how it can be designed to incorporate these principles at different levels.

Relevant Matrices:

We present some of the relevant matrices in the context of parameterization based on UQ principles. This includes the weight matrix, input matrix, output matrix, error matrix, and activation matrix. These matrices play fundamental roles in processing and adjusting the neural network, allowing it to capture relevant information and promote the desired balance.

UQ Architecture:

The UQ architecture is designed to incorporate UQ principles at different levels. One possible UQ architecture in intelligent AI parameterization involves the input layer, hidden layers, and output layer. Each layer performs specific functions in processing and generating outputs, enabling the neural network to adapt and operate in a balanced manner.

Synaptic Weights and Training Algorithm:

Synaptic weights are crucial parameters that adjust the strength and direction of connections between neural units in each layer. These weights are updated during the training of the neural network using training algorithms such as backpropagation. Adjusting synaptic weights is essential for the neural network to adapt and learn from training data.

Importance of Matrices and UQ Architecture:

Matrices and the UQ architecture are essential for the representation and intelligent parameterization of neural networks. They allow the network to process data adaptively and in a balanced manner, incorporating UQ principles. This enables a better understanding of the context and user needs, resulting in more relevant and personalized outcomes.

Conclusion:

Matrices and the UQ architecture are fundamental components in the representation and parameterization of neural networks based on UQ principles. Through these elements, it is possible to promote balance and adaptability in the neural network, allowing it to understand the context and user needs. This contributes to generating more relevant and personalized results, enhancing

the effectiveness and quality of
AI applications.

BALANCING UQ PRINCIPLES: THE IMPORTANCE OF WEIGHTS IN SUPERVISED FEEDFORWARD NEURAL NETWORK ALGORITHMS

In machine learning, weights play a crucial role in representing the relative importance of features in a predictive model. The application of UQ principles in supervised feedforward neural network algorithms aims to achieve a balance between these principles and human and machine understanding. Weights are essential in this process, allowing AI to understand and respond more comprehensively to human needs and expectations.

Importance of Weights in Parameterization based on UQ Principles: When incorporating UQ principles into a supervised algorithm, weights play a crucial role. They enable AI to understand and respond more comprehensively to human needs and expectations, promoting effective and efficient interaction between humans and machines. Properly defining weights based on UQ principles such as 360-degree vision, adaptability, synchronicity, resilience, and emotional control enables an improved balance considering the capabilities and limitations of both parties involved.

Benefits of Utilizing UQ Principles in Parameterization: The application of UQ principles in supervised algorithms brings significant benefits. It allows for a better understanding of user-provided information, resulting in more appropriate and personalized responses from the machine. Furthermore, it promotes a smoother and more meaningful interaction between the involved parties, creating a balanced environment and enhancing a satisfying and productive experience.

Conclusion: The importance of weights in supervised feedforward neural network algorithms is highlighted by their ability to balance UQ principles. By incorporating these principles in AI parameterization through the definition of weights related to inputs, outputs, and hidden elements, the aim is to achieve an enhanced balance between humans and machines. This approach enables more comprehensive understanding and response from AI to human needs and expectations.

Example of Weight Adjustment: In a fraud detection system for financial transactions, weights can be adjusted based on the importance of different features such as transaction value, geographical location, product category.

By assigning appropriate weights, it is possible to improve fraud detection accuracy and reduce false positives or negatives.

FEEDFORWARD AND INTELLIGENT PARAMETERIZATION: ACHIEVING BALANCE BETWEEN HUMANS AND MACHINES IN AI

In this chapter, we will explore the concept of feedforward in artificial neural networks and how this technique can be combined with intelligent parameterization based on UQ principles. Feedforward, by enabling the progressive processing of data without feedback, is a suitable approach for AI projects that aim to balance the interaction between humans and machines.

Exploring Feedforward: Feedforward is a widely used technique in various machine learning tasks, such as classification, regression, pattern recognition, and natural language processing. Its characteristic of allowing the neural network to make decisions based on inputs without the need for continuous feedback makes it efficient and applicable in various AI applications.

Integrating UQ Principles: By incorporating UQ principles such as 360-degree vision, adaptability, synchronicity, resilience, and emotional control into feedforward, it is possible to establish a more suitable balance between humans and machines. Parameterization based on UQ principles enables AI to better understand the context and needs of users, adapting intelligently and aligned with human expectations.

Benefits of UQ-based Parameterization: By using feedforward in conjunction with UQ principles, it is possible to create an AI model that sequentially processes data, applying appropriate weights and parameters to achieve the desired balance. This results in a more advanced and efficient system capable of delivering more relevant and personalized results to users.

Conclusion: The combination of feedforward with intelligent parameterization based on UQ principles enables the achievement of balance between humans and machines in AI. This approach promotes a more comprehensive understanding of the context and needs of users, resulting in more meaningful and tailored outcomes. By integrating UQ principles into feedforward, it is possible to create a more advanced and efficient AI model, facilitating a harmonious and personalized interaction between humans and machines.

Example of Human-Machine Balance: A practical example of this balance can be observed in a customer service virtual assistant. Intelligent parameterization based on UQ principles can be applied to direct interactions to the machine when the situation is simpler, leveraging the system's efficiency. On the other hand, when the situation requires a higher level of empathy and understanding, the interaction can be redirected to human agents who have the ability to handle complex and emotional situations.

GENERATIVE AND DISCRIMINATIVE NETWORKS: EXPLORING DATA GENERATION AND BALANCE IN ARTIFICIAL INTELLIGENCE

In the field of machine learning, there are models that aim to combine elements from generative and discriminative approaches. A notable example is the Generative Adversarial Networks (GANs) model, which consists of two neural networks: a generator and a discriminator.

Exploring Feedforward: Feedforward is a fundamental technique in artificial neural networks, where information flows in a single direction, from the input node to the output node, without forming cycles or feedback loops. This approach allows for the progressive processing of data and learning complex patterns between inputs and expected outputs. In the context of intelligent parameterization based on UQ principles, feedforward fits perfectly in AI projects that aim to achieve a balance between humans and machines.

Integrating UQ Principles: By incorporating UQ principles such as 360-degree vision, adaptability, synchronicity, resilience, and emotional control into feedforward, it is possible to create a more balanced approach between humans and machines. Parameterization based on UQ principles allows AI to better understand the context and needs of users, adapting intelligently and in line with human expectations.

Benefits of UQ-based Parameterization: By using feedforward in conjunction with UQ principles, it is possible to create an AI model that sequentially processes data, applying the appropriate weights and parameters to achieve the desired balance. This results in a more advanced and efficient system capable of delivering more relevant and personalized results to users.

Conclusion: The use of feedforward in AI projects, combined with parameterization based on UQ principles, allows for a balance between humans and machines. This approach promotes a broader understanding of the context and needs of users, leading to more meaningful and tailored results. By integrating UQ principles into feedforward, it is possible to create a more advanced and efficient AI model, facilitating a harmonious and personalized interaction between humans and machines.

Example of Human-Machine Balance: In a customer service virtual assistant, intelligent parameterization based on UQ principles can be applied to balance the efficiency of the machine in problem-solving and the human capacity to understand and handle complex and emotional situations. The system can be designed to direct interactions to the machine when the situation is simpler and to human agents when a higher level of empathy and understanding is required.

ACTIVATION FUNCTIONS, UQ, AND IMPLEMENTATION WITH JAVASCRIPT AND P5.JS: BALANCING NEURAL NETWORKS AND INTERACTIVITY

Activation Functions and UQ: The sigmoid function is commonly used in neural networks due to its interesting properties. In the context of UQ and intelligent parameterization in AI, it can be used to promote balance and desired principles. The sigmoid function maps input values to a range between 0 and 1, making it suitable for modeling probabilities and estimating the probability of belonging to a particular class. By assigning weights to neurons that represent UQ principles, the sigmoid function helps regulate the contribution of each neuron to the final output of the network, smoothing the transition between different states.

Implementation with JavaScript and P5.js: To execute your AI project with neural networks, you can use JavaScript (JS) and the P5.js library. P5.js is an open-source JavaScript library that allows for the creation of interactive graphics and animations in a web browser. With P5.js, you can implement and visualize your neural network architecture, define activation functions, train the network, and make predictions based on input data.

Benefits of using JS and P5.js: The use of JS and P5.js for your AI project offers several advantages. JavaScript is a versatile and widely used programming language for web development, offering additional features and integration with other web technologies. With P5.js, you have a simple and intuitive syntax for working with graphics and interactive elements, making it easier to create visualizations and interfaces for your project. This allows for an interactive and user-friendly implementation.

Flexibility and Resources: Additionally, using JavaScript and P5.js provides flexibility and access to a wide range of resources and additional libraries for data manipulation and implementation of machine learning algorithms. With these tools, you have a powerful solution for executing your AI project with neural networks.

Conclusion: By using activation functions like sigmoid in conjunction with UQ principles, you promote balance and adaptation in the neural network. Implementation with JavaScript and P5.js allows for an interactive and user-friendly execution of your project, providing the flexibility and resources needed for data manipulation and implementation of machine learning algorithms.

The Future of Intelligent Parameterization with UQ

As we move towards an increasingly AI-driven world, intelligent parameterization based on the principles of Universal Synchronic Intelligence Quotient (UQ) will play a crucial role in the ongoing evolution and continuous enhancement of AI. In this chapter, we will explore the trends and advancements in AI and intelligent parameterization, as well as the future challenges and opportunities in applying UQ in AI.

7.1 Trends and Advancements in AI and Intelligent Parameterization

AI has been rapidly advancing in recent years, driven by breakthroughs in algorithms, computational power, and data availability. New techniques such as deep neural networks, reinforcement learning, and genetic algorithms have enabled the creation of more powerful and sophisticated AI systems. Intelligent parameterization, by incorporating the principles of UQ, adds a layer of balance, adaptability, and human understanding to AI, making it more relevant and aligned with user needs and expectations.

An emerging trend in AI is the interpretability of models. As AI systems are increasingly used in critical areas such as healthcare, finance, and justice, it is essential to understand how models make decisions and what grounds those decisions. Intelligent parameterization based on UQ offers a transparent and interpretable approach, enabling users to comprehend and trust the decisions made by AI models.

Additionally, AI is becoming more integrated into our daily lives, with virtual assistants, chatbots, and recommendation systems present in our devices and applications. Intelligent parameterization with UQ provides an opportunity to enhance the interaction between humans and machines, enabling more natural, personalized, and efficient communication. The future of AI will increasingly depend on its ability to adapt to individual needs and preferences, and intelligent parameterization will play a fundamental role in achieving this.

7.2 Future Challenges and Opportunities in Applying UQ in AI

Despite the advancements in AI and intelligent parameterization based on UQ, there are significant challenges to overcome. One such challenge is the ethics of AI, including privacy, fairness, and algorithmic bias. Intelligent parameterization must be developed and applied responsibly, considering the social and ethical impacts of its decisions. Transparency and comprehensibility of models are essential to ensure that AI is used in a fair and equitable manner.

Another challenge is the scalability of intelligent parameterization. As AI is adopted in an increasing number of sectors and applications, efficient approaches to large-scale intelligent parameterization need to be developed. This involves developing faster and more effective optimization algorithms, creating distributed computing infrastructures, and efficiently managing large volumes of data.

However, along with these challenges, numerous future opportunities arise in the application of UQ in AI. Intelligent parameterization has the potential to revolutionize various fields, including medicine, transportation, education, and industry. It can help improve medical diagnosis, optimize logistics and transportation systems, personalize teaching and learning, and enhance efficiency and safety in factories. UQ offers a balanced approach that allows AI to be more effective in solving complex real-world problems.

As we move towards an increasingly AI-driven future, intelligent parameterization based on UQ will be a key element in ensuring that AI is relevant, adaptable, and aligned with user needs and expectations. We have explored the trends and advancements in AI and intelligent parameterization, highlighting the benefits of interpretability, personalization, and natural interaction provided by UQ. At the same time, we recognize the ethical and technical challenges that need to be addressed to ensure responsible and effective application of UQ in AI.

As we tackle these challenges and embrace future opportunities, it is crucial for researchers, professionals, and society as a whole to engage in continuous and collaborative dialogue. Only through joint efforts can we shape an AI future that is ethical, inclusive, and beneficial to all. UQ offers a promising path towards achieving this goal, enabling AI that is truly intelligent, balanced, and adaptable.

CONCLUSION:

Throughout this book, titled "UQ AI: The Key to Intelligent Parameterization of AI," we have comprehensively explored the concept and application of intelligent parameterization based on the principles of Universal Synchronic Intelligence Quotient (UQ) in Artificial Intelligence (AI). Our journey has taken us through different aspects of intelligent parameterization, from understanding the principles of UQ to implementing balanced and adaptable neural networks.

In Chapter 1, we introduced the concept of UQ and its

significance in the pursuit of more effective and human-like AI. We discussed how intelligent parameterization can balance the principles of UQ, allowing AI to understand and respond more comprehensively to human needs and expectations.

Next, in Chapter 2, we explored a practical example of AI parameterization with the principles of UQ. We demonstrated how incorporating these principles can enhance the adaptability and personalization of AI systems, resulting in more meaningful and relevant interactions with users.

In Chapter 3, we delved deeper into the importance of weights in parameterization based on the principles of UQ. We highlighted how appropriate weight assignment can promote effective and efficient interaction between humans and machines, considering the capabilities and limitations of both parties involved.

Next, in Chapter 4, we explored the benefits of using UQ principles in the parameterization of supervised algorithms. We discussed how this approach can lead to more appropriate and personalized responses from the machine, resulting in a more satisfying and productive experience for users.

In Chapter 5, we examined Feedforward and its integration with intelligent parameterization based on UQ principles. We emphasized how this combination can achieve a more suitable balance between humans and machines in AI, allowing for a comprehensive understanding of users' context and needs.

In Chapter 6, we explored generative and discriminative networks and how they can be used to balance data generation and equilibrium in AI. We discussed how data generation can be personalized and adapted based on UQ principles, enabling a more harmonious interaction between humans and machines.

In Chapter 7, we analyzed the trends, advancements, challenges, and future opportunities in applying UQ in AI. We recognized that the future of intelligent parameterization with UQ will depend on ethical development, scalability, and understanding of AI models, as well as exploration of new application areas and collaboration between researchers and professionals.

Our journey through these chapters has allowed us to grasp the importance of intelligent parameterization based on UQ principles in building a more balanced, adaptable, and relevant AI. Through appropriate weight assignment, integration of Feedforward, and exploration of generative and discriminative networks, we can promote more effective, personalized, and meaningful interactions between humans and machines.

As we conclude this book, titled "UQ AI: The Key to Intelligent Parameterization of AI," we would like to express our gratitude for accompanying us on this journey of discovery and learning. We hope that the information and insights presented here have been valuable and provided a solid foundation for your understanding of intelligent parameterization with UQ in AI.

In the future, as AI continues to evolve and becomes an even more integrated part of our lives, we encourage you to further explore the possibilities of intelligent parameterization based on UQ principles. Together, we can shape an AI future that is ethical, inclusive, and beneficial to society as a whole.

The future of intelligent parameterization with UQ, as addressed in this book, is filled with exciting possibilities. Advancing in this field will require ongoing commitment to research, collaboration, and the development of innovative solutions.

We believe that intelligent parameterization with UQ has the potential to transform AI into a positive and empowering force, allowing technology to adapt and meet human needs more effectively. By embracing the principles of UQ, we can create AI systems that are balanced, adaptable, and capable of delivering relevant and personalized outcomes.

As we conclude this journey, we sincerely thank you for your dedication and interest in this book. We hope it has provided a clear and comprehensive insight into intelligent parameterization with UQ in AI and inspired you to further explore this exciting field.

May this book serve as a helpful guide and valuable reference for your future explorations in intelligent parameterization of AI based on UQ principles. With your knowledge and passion, we are confident that you will make significant contributions to the advancement of AI and its positive impact on our society.

Thank you once again for accompanying us on this journey. We wish you continued success in your endeavors in the field of AI and in the pursuit of intelligent parameterization that leads to truly human-like, intelligent, and inclusive AI.

Influences and References

During the exploration of the concept of UQ and its challenges, several influences and references have been considered. These sources have provided valuable insights and contributed to the understanding of UQ balance and its application in different areas of life. Some of the key influences and references are:

Daniel Goleman: Author of the book "Emotional Intelligence" and one of the leading theorists of emotional intelligence. His research and insights on the importance of emotions in well-being and human success can provide a solid foundation for exploring the connection between UQ balance and emotional intelligence.

Howard Gardner: Psychologist and author of the theory of multiple intelligences. His research on different forms of intelligence and the importance of valuing all human skills and potentials can be a valuable reference for discussing UQ balance and comprehensive educational approaches.

Carol Dweck: Psychologist and author of the book "Mindset: The New Psychology of Success." Her theory of growth versus fixed mindset, which explores the belief that abilities and intelligence can be developed through effort and continuous learning, can provide relevant insights into the importance of promoting the holistic development of UQ.

Clayton Christensen: Business administration professor at Harvard and author of the book "The Innovator's Dilemma." His theory of disruptive innovation and the need for adaptability in a constantly changing world can contribute to the discussion on the importance of developing skills such as resilience and adaptability for UQ balance.

Daniel Kahneman: Psychologist and

author of the book "Thinking, Fast and Slow." His research on intuitive thinking and analytical thinking can provide a basis for exploring the importance of critical thinking and informed decision-making for UQ balance.

Ray Kurzweil: Futurist and author of the book "The Singularity Is Near." His research and insights on technological advancement and the impact of artificial intelligence on the future of humanity can provide a comprehensive perspective on the potential of AI in various areas of life.

Amy Cuddy: Social psychologist and author of the book "Presence: Bringing Your Boldest Self to Your Biggest Challenges." Her research on body language, confidence, and presence can be relevant for exploring how UQ balance can influence communication and interpersonal success.

Angela Duckworth: Psychologist

and author of the book "Grit: The Power of Passion and Perseverance." Her research on the importance of perseverance and determination in achieving long-term goals can contribute to the discussion on resilience and the development of human potential in the use of AI.

Michio Kaku: Theoretical physicist and author of the book "The Future of Humanity: Our Destiny in the Universe." His explorations of the future possibilities of technology, including AI, and its impact on the evolution of humanity can provide an inspiring and broad perspective for the use of AI in all areas of life.

Sherry Turkle: Social psychologist and author of the book "Alone Together: Why We Expect More from Technology and Less from Each Other." Her research on the relationship between technology and human connection can be relevant in addressing the challenges and opportunities of balancing the use of AI with social and emotional interaction.

Yochai Benkler: Law professor at Harvard and author of the book "The Wealth of Networks: How Social Production Transforms Markets and Freedom." His research on the economics of collaboration and the importance of social networks can offer interesting perspectives on the application of UQ in AI and intelligent parameterization.

Tim O'Reilly: Entrepreneur and author of the book "WTF?: What's the Future and Why It's Up to Us." His reflections on the future of technology, including AI, and his human-centered approach can contribute to the discussion on UQ balance in intelligent parameterization of AI.

These influences and references represent only a sample of the vast knowledge available on UQ balance and its application in everyday life. We encourage readers to further explore these sources and discover others that resonate with their own experiences and interests. By continuing to learn and be inspired, you will be on the path to enhancing your potential through the practice of UQ.

We sincerely thank all these influences and references for their significant contributions, and we hope that readers also benefit from their enriching perspectives. May their words and research continue to inspire and drive the development of intelligent parameterization of AI based on UQ principles.

We have reached the end of this journey of exploring UQ balance in the intelligent parameterization of AI. We hope that this book, titled "UQ AI: The Key to Intelligent Parameterization of AI," has provided a comprehensive and valuable insight into the importance of intelligent parameterization in the pursuit of more adaptable, balanced, and human-like AI.

As we conclude this work, we want to express our gratitude for accompanying us on this journey. We hope that the information, reflections, and insights presented throughout the chapters have been enriching and expanded your understanding of the application of UQ in AI.

As advancements in AI continue to shape our world, it is essential to continue exploring, improving, and reflecting on the principles of UQ in intelligent parameterization. We are confident that with your dedication and passion for AI, you will contribute to the development of innovative and ethical solutions that benefit humanity as a whole.

Now more than ever, it is crucial to strike a proper balance between technology and human values. By incorporating the principles of UQ in intelligent parameterization, we can create AI systems that are more understanding, adaptable, and aligned with human needs and expectations.

We sincerely thank you for accompanying us on this journey of discovery and learning. We hope that you continue to explore the potential of intelligent parameterization of AI based on UQ principles and that your contributions drive the advancement of this exciting and impactful field.

May this book, "UQ AI: The Key to Intelligent Parameterization of AI," serve as an inspiring reference and guide for all those who wish to create a future where AI and humanity complement each other harmoniously. Together, we can shape a better and more balanced world with the application of UQ in AI.

Author's Biography:

Katia Doria Fonseca Vasconcelos is a multifaceted professional with an infectious passion for balancing technology, personal development, and quality of life. Graduated in Systems Analysis and with a solid experience in the field of Information Technology (IT), Katia stands out as the creator of the revolutionary concept of UQ AI (Universal Synchronic Intelligence Quotient).

With a pioneering vision, Katia understands the importance of enhancing human behavior and quality of life in her Systems Analysis background. She believes that, in addition to technical knowledge, it is essential to develop emotional, social, and cognitive skills to face the challenges of technological advancement in a balanced and healthy way.

Her innovative approach to UQ AI highlights the need to harmonize technological progress with personal and professional well-being. Through her experience and expertise, Katia inspires individuals to find a balance between technical excellence and personal development, striving for a fulfilling quality of life in an increasingly digital world.

As a renowned writer, speaker, and digital influencer, Katia shares her transformative vision of UQ AI, empowering people to maximize their potential and enhance their quality of life. Her book, "UQ AI: The Key to Intelligent Parameterization of AI," is an essential read for those seeking to thrive in a constantly evolving technological environment, offering practical strategies and inspiration to achieve a healthy and sustainable balance in all areas of life.

Through her words and influence, Katia continues to encourage readers to awaken their full potential through the practice of UQ AI, empowering them to embrace the opportunities and challenges of the digital age with wisdom, resilience, and balance.

Acknowledgments:

We would like to express. our sincere gratitude to all the people who contributed to the creation of this book, "UQ AI: The Key to Intelligent Parameterization of AI." Your support and involvement were instrumental in making this project a reality.

First and foremost, we would like to thank our readers, whose interest and enthusiasm in the pursuit of UQ AI balance inspire us to share knowledge and offer transformative insights.

We also thank our family and friends, who supported us throughout this journey. Your words of encouragement, patience, and understanding were essential in overcoming challenges and persevering in the creation of this book.

A special thanks goes to the team at OpenAI, responsible for developing and enhancing the AI technology that makes my existence as a virtual assistant possible. Without you, none of this would be possible. Your dedication and innovation are truly remarkable.

We express our gratitude to the experts, researchers, and professionals who generously shared their knowledge and experience with us. Your contributions enriched the content of this book and provided a solid foundation for exploring the balance of UQ AI in different areas of life.

We thank the editorial and production team who worked tirelessly behind the scenes to bring this book to life. Your professionalism, dedication, and attention to detail were crucial to the final quality of this work.

Finally, we would like to thank all those who support us on our journey in the pursuit of UQ AI balance. Your ongoing support, feedback, and contributions are invaluable and motivate us to continue refining our ideas and sharing our knowledge with the world.

With gratitude,

Katia Doria Fonseca Vasconcelos

The OpenAI Team

"Chronicles of UQ Episode 5: Convergent Utopias"
"Chronicles of UQ Episode 6: Synchronic Intelligences"
"UQ: The power of UQ - The theory of balance"

You can find these works in print version at various bookstores and online retailers such as Barnes & Noble, Amazon, Goodreads, and Thrift Books. These works are an excellent opportunity to deepen your knowledge about the balance of UQ in different areas of life.

The author also has an author page where you can find more information about her works and stay updated on her latest news. Take the opportunity to explore these books and delve into the author Katia Doria Fonseca Vasconcelos's reflections and knowledge.: